This planner belongs to:

If found please return to:

Email:

Telephone Number:

INTRODUCTION

If you have ever been on a commercial flight, then you have heard the safety instructions. One of the most important things they note is to make sure you put your own mask on before you help others.

Why?

If you don't take care of your own needs, you won't be able to fully help other people as and when you want to.

This is the key to self-care as well. If you aren't taking care of yourself, how can you expect to watch over the people you love?

All too often we're busy and stressed. There's just too much going on in the day and we're already short on time. We're not as fine as we like to pretend we are. If we're honest, we're probably not spending as much time on ourselves as we ought to. In short, we're neglecting self-care. If you think self-care isn't a big deal, then consider the statistics that show that many of us are either chronically dehydrated, not getting enough sleep, feel tired before we even get to work or are feeling anxious or depressed...or maybe all of those things!

If you just winced from reading this list, you're not alone. No, we are not fine, and it's time we did something about it.

This journal gives you exercises to work through and space for planning and reflecting on your self-care practices for the next 12 weeks. Using this journal every day for the next 12 weeks brings the biggest changes, but you can fill in this journal at any rate that works for you as it is undated.

"Love yourself first, because that's who you'll be spending the rest of your life with." - LW

WHY SELF-CARE

Why is it so hard to take care of ourselves? The answer could be found in our own compassion. We spend so much time worrying about those we love and making sure we meet our responsibilities, we forget about a very basic truth.

We cannot fully take care of anyone else, unless we are in a position to do so. What does this mean? Think about what can happen when self-care suffers. Do any of these sound familiar?

· You have a harder time thinking.
· You're sick more often.
· You feel overwhelmed.
· You wake up tired, even after a full night of sleep.
· You forget what you're about to say.
· You find yourself isolating and avoiding social situations.
· You're cranky or feel "off" and may snap at people.
· Simple tasks seem to take a lot of effort.
· You're dragging yourself through the day.
· Decisions become really difficult, even simple ones.
· You're worried or anxious though you're not sure why.
· You're not eating right, either too much or too little.
· You're ignoring things you used to enjoy, either through lack of interest or energy.

Now think about what this means when it comes to taking care of others. How in the world are you supposed to take care of any outside responsibilities, even ones you love such as taking care of your kids, when you're feeling like that? It doesn't really work, does it? Worse, we're not doing what's right by the one person who's supposed to matter more than anything: **YOU!**

"Today is your first step towards nurturing your body, mind and soul " - LW

WHAT SELF-CARE CAN DO FOR YOU

As you read through the next sections, I want you to really think about what you're reading. Imagine this journal as being part of your journey to better self-care. See how the changes come together to form a picture of a new, and rather different you, one that experiences life a little differently than what we saw listed at the beginning of the chapter.

With better mental and physical health you could:

· Have no trouble thinking.
· Wake up feeling rested.
· Look forward to what comes next with enthusiasm.
· Be articulate and well-spoken.
· Never miss a deadline.
· Enjoy a great social life.
· Be in a great mood.
· Be patient with those around you.
· Handle complex tasks with ease.
· Feel like you can keep going all day long.
· Feel relaxed and calm.
· Feel full of enthusiasm, every single day.

Sound pretty good? Then what are you waiting for?

"Today I decided to say YES to prioritising ME!"

- LW

SELF-CARE IDEAS

HERE ARE SOME SELF-CARE IDEAS.
HIGHLIGHT ANY THAT APPEAL TO YOU AND
ADD YOUR OWN IDEAS ON THE NEXT PAGE.

Meditate	Enjoy healthy food	Exercise
Nap	Read a book	Buy a new outfit
Have a massage	Have a relaxing bath/shower	Listen to your fave podcast
Call a friend	Take a course	Do some gardening
Enjoy a treat	Watch a movie	Get your hair styled
Repeat an affirmation	Make something	Get a manicure
Buy yourself flowers	Laugh	Get an early night
Plan a getaway	Bake	Cuddle your pet

SELF-CARE IDEAS

SELF-CARE PRACTICE IS DOING ANYTHING THAT YOU LOVE! JOT DOWN YOUR IDEAS BELOW.

A LETTER TO MYSELF

Dear _____,

It's time. I am finally ready to let go of the old, commit to myself and embrace change.

I believe that the world is transformed by the choices we make and I know that my life is important. My words, thoughts and actions are powerful.

So I am willing to become more _____ and choose to do more _____.

I am committed to releasing my old stories about who I am and what I am capable of because _____.

In the coming months, I am going to be the most _____ person I know and I'm going to spend more time with _____, _____, _____ doing things like _____, _____, & _____.

I am also going to commit to spending less time doing things that waste my precious time like _____, _____, & _____ because they make me _____.

The top three things that are most important to me are.....
1.
2.
3.
.......and I am ready to make them a priority. No matter what life brings.

One last thing: I love you and appreciate you _____, because of all of the amazing things you have made it through and all the incredible things you have accomplished. Especially that time you _____.

I truly wish for you all the health, wealth and happiness in the world.

I believe in me.

INTENTIONS

STEP #1: YOUR WHY STATEMENT. Take some time to write down why you have chosen to embark on this self-care journal and take this journey.

STEP #2: YOUR JOURNAL INTENTIONS. Take a deep breath and write down how you feel about your mind, body and spirit now. Then write down how you want to feel instead.

HOW I FEEL IN MY **MIND:**	HOW I WANT TO FEEL:**MIND**

HOW I FEEL IN MY **BODY:**	HOW I WANT TO FEEL:**BODY**

HOW I FEEL IN MY **SPIRIT:**	HOW I WANT TO FEEL:**SPIRIT**

AFFIRMATIONS

Here are some ideas for your daily affirmations. Play around with them and make them your own.

I am enough

I am worthy

I am creative

I am strong

I can achieve anything

I am loved

I am healthy, wealthy and wise

I am beautiful inside and out

Today is going to be a great day

I am abundant

I attract good people into my life

Exciting things are coming my way

I am confident

I am safe

I am supported

The universe has my back

Today I choose happiness

I radiate love and compassion

I set healthy boundaries

I take time to nurture my body, mind and soul

I am successful

HOW TO USE THIS JOURNAL

Simply turn to the following pages and fill in the simple-to-use intentions, gratitude and journaling pages every single day!

Record The Date And Day

Rate Your Mood

Record Your Sleep

Check Off Self-Care Practices Completed and add your own

Record Your Affirmation Of The Day

Reminder List

Morning Intention Prompts

Evening Reflection Prompts

Write 3 Things You're Grateful For

Free Journaling Page To Continue From The Prompted Page

Weekly Win Prompts

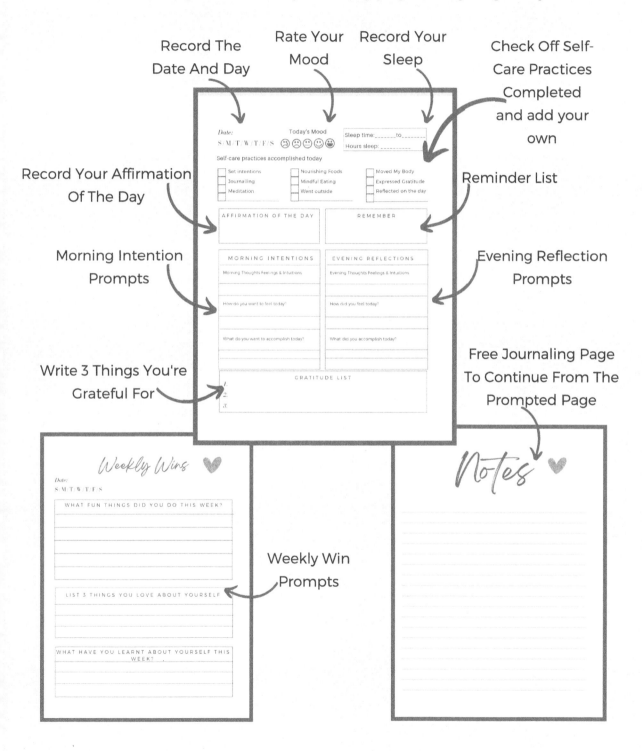

Date:
S/M/T/W/T/F/S   Today's Mood   Sleep time:_____to_____
                                 Hours sleep: _____

Self-care practices accomplished today

- [ ] Set intentions   - [ ] Nourishing Foods   - [ ] Moved My Body
- [ ] Journalling   - [ ] Mindful Eating   - [ ] Expressed Gratitude
- [ ] Meditation   - [ ] Went outside   - [ ] Reflected on the day

AFFIRMATION OF THE DAY   REMEMBER

MORNING INTENTIONS   EVENING REFLECTIONS
Morning Thoughts Feelings & Intuitions   Evening Thoughts Feelings & Intuitions

How do you want to feel today?   How did you feel today?

What do you want to accomplish today?   What did you accomplish today?

GRATITUDE LIST
1.
2.
3.

Weekly Wins ♥
Date:
S/M/T/W/T/F/S

WHAT FUN THINGS DID YOU DO THIS WEEK?

LIST 3 THINGS YOU LOVE ABOUT YOURSELF

WHAT HAVE YOU LEARNT ABOUT YOURSELF THIS WEEK?

Notes ♥

Date:

S / M / T / W / T / F / S

Today's Mood ☹ ☹ 😐 🙂 😃

Sleep time:_____to_____

Hours slept: _____

Self-care practices accomplished today

- [ ] Set intentions
- [ ] Journaling
- [ ] Meditation

- [ ] Nourishing Foods
- [ ] Mindful Eating
- [ ] Went outside

- [ ] Moved My Body
- [ ] Expressed Gratitude
- [ ] Reflected on the day

AFFIRMATION OF THE DAY

REMEMBER

MORNING INTENTIONS

Morning Thoughts Feelings & Intuitions

How do you want to feel today?

What do you want to accomplish today?

EVENING REFLECTIONS

Evening Thoughts Feelings & Intuitions

How did you feel today?

What did you accomplish today?

GRATITUDE LIST

1.

2.

3.

Notes

Believe in yourself

Date:

S / M / T / W / T / F / S

Today's Mood

😟 😖 😐 🙂 😄

Sleep time:_____to_____

Hours slept: _____

Self-care practices accomplished today

- [ ] Set intentions
- [ ] Journaling
- [ ] Meditation

- [ ] Nourishing Foods
- [ ] Mindful Eating
- [ ] Went outside

- [ ] Moved My Body
- [✓] Expressed Gratitude
- [ ] Reflected on the day

AFFIRMATION OF THE DAY	REMEMBER

MORNING INTENTIONS

Morning Thoughts Feelings & Intuitions

How do you want to feel today?

What do you want to accomplish today?

EVENING REFLECTIONS

Evening Thoughts Feelings & Intuitions

How did you feel today?

What did you accomplish today?

GRATITUDE LIST

1.
2.
3.

Notes

You've got this!

Date:

S / M / T / W / T / F / S

Today's Mood

😖 😞 😐 🙂 😃

Sleep time:_____to_____

Hours slept: _____

Self-care practices accomplished today

☐ Set intentions
☐ Journaling
☐ Meditation
☐

☐ Nourishing Foods
☐ Mindful Eating
☐ Went outside
☐

☐ Moved My Body
☐ Expressed Gratitude
☐ Reflected on the day
☐

AFFIRMATION OF THE DAY

REMEMBER

MORNING INTENTIONS

Morning Thoughts Feelings & Intuitions

How do you want to feel today?

What do you want to accomplish today?

EVENING REFLECTIONS

Evening Thoughts Feelings & Intuitions

How did you feel today?

What did you accomplish today?

GRATITUDE LIST

1.

2.

3.

Notes

Don't stop now, keep going

Date:

S / M / T / W / T / F / S

Today's Mood

☹ ☹ 😐 ☺ ☺

Sleep time:_____to_____

Hours slept: _____

Self-care practices accomplished today

- ☐ Set intentions
- ☐ Journaling
- ☐ Meditation

- ☐ Nourishing Foods
- ☐ Mindful Eating
- ☐ Went outside

- ☐ Moved My Body
- ☐ Expressed Gratitude
- ☐ Reflected on the day

AFFIRMATION OF THE DAY

REMEMBER

MORNING INTENTIONS

Morning Thoughts Feelings & Intuitions

How do you want to feel today?

What do you want to accomplish today?

EVENING REFLECTIONS

Evening Thoughts Feelings & Intuitions

How did you feel today?

What did you accomplish today?

GRATITUDE LIST

1.

2.

3.

Notes

Things will get better

Date:

S / M / T / W / T / F / S

Today's Mood

☹ ☹ 😐 🙂 😄

Sleep time:_____to_____

Hours slept: _____

Self-care practices accomplished today

☐ Set intentions

☐ Journaling

☐ Meditation

☐

☐ Nourishing Foods

☐ Mindful Eating

☐ Went outside

☐

☐ Moved My Body

☐ Expressed Gratitude

☐ Reflected on the day

☐

AFFIRMATION OF THE DAY

REMEMBER

MORNING INTENTIONS

Morning Thoughts Feelings & Intuitions

How do you want to feel today?

What do you want to accomplish today?

EVENING REFLECTIONS

Evening Thoughts Feelings & Intuitions

How did you feel today?

What did you accomplish today?

GRATITUDE LIST

1.

2.

3.

Notes

You are magical

Date:

S/M/T/W/T/F/S

Today's Mood

😣 😞 😐 🙂 😃

Sleep time:_____to_____

Hours slept: _____

Self-care practices accomplished today

- [ ] Set intentions
- [ ] Journaling
- [ ] Meditation

- [ ] Nourishing Foods
- [ ] Mindful Eating
- [ ] Went outside

- [ ] Moved My Body
- [ ] Expressed Gratitude
- [ ] Reflected on the day

AFFIRMATION OF THE DAY	REMEMBER

MORNING INTENTIONS

Morning Thoughts Feelings & Intuitions

How do you want to feel today?

What do you want to accomplish today?

EVENING REFLECTIONS

Evening Thoughts Feelings & Intuitions

How did you feel today?

What did you accomplish today?

GRATITUDE LIST

1.

2.

3.

Notes

Choose your happiness today

Date:

S / M / T / W / T / F / S

Today's Mood

☹ ☹ 😐 🙂 😊

Sleep time:_____to_____

Hours slept: _____

Self-care practices accomplished today

☐ Set intentions
☐ Journaling
☐ Meditation

☐ Nourishing Foods
☐ Mindful Eating
☐ Went outside

☐ Moved My Body
☐ Expressed Gratitude
☐ Reflected on the day

AFFIRMATION OF THE DAY

REMEMBER

MORNING INTENTIONS

Morning Thoughts Feelings & Intuitions

How do you want to feel today?

What do you want to accomplish today?

EVENING REFLECTIONS

Evening Thoughts Feelings & Intuitions

How did you feel today?

What did you accomplish today?

GRATITUDE LIST

1.

2.

3.

Notes

All of the answers are inside you

Weekly Wins

Date:

S / M / T / W / T / F / S

WHAT WERE THE BEST MOMENTS OF THE WEEK?

GIVE YOURSELF A COMPLIMENT

WHAT SELF-CARE PRACTICES DID YOU LOVE DOING THIS WEEK?

Date:

S / M / T / W / T / F / S

Today's Mood

😞 😣 😐 🙂 😃

Sleep time:_____to_____

Hours slept: _____

Self-care practices accomplished today

☐ Set intentions
☐ Journaling
☐ Meditation

☐ Nourishing Foods
☐ Mindful Eating
☐ Went outside

☐ Moved My Body
☐ Expressed Gratitude
☐ Reflected on the day

AFFIRMATION OF THE DAY

REMEMBER

MORNING INTENTIONS

Morning Thoughts Feelings & Intuitions

How do you want to feel today?

What do you want to accomplish today?

EVENING REFLECTIONS

Evening Thoughts Feelings & Intuitions

How did you feel today?

What did you accomplish today?

GRATITUDE LIST

1.

2.

3.

Notes

You are the leader of your own life

Date:

S / M / T / W / T / F / S

Today's Mood

☹ ☹ 😐 🙂 😄

Sleep time:_____to_____

Hours slept: _____

Self-care practices accomplished today

☐ Set intentions
☐ Journaling
☐ Meditation
☐

☐ Nourishing Foods
☐ Mindful Eating
☐ Went outside
☐

☐ Moved My Body
☐ Expressed Gratitude
☐ Reflected on the day
☐

AFFIRMATION OF THE DAY

REMEMBER

MORNING INTENTIONS

Morning Thoughts Feelings & Intuitions

How do you want to feel today?

What do you want to accomplish today?

EVENING REFLECTIONS

Evening Thoughts Feelings & Intuitions

How did you feel today?

What did you accomplish today?

GRATITUDE LIST

1.

2.

3.

Notes

Keep shining brightly

Date:

S / M / T / W / T / F / S

Today's Mood

😟 😞 😐 🙂 😊

Sleep time:_____to_____

Hours slept: _____

Self-care practices accomplished today

☐ Set intentions
☐ Journaling
☐ Meditation

☐ Nourishing Foods
☐ Mindful Eating
☐ Went outside

☐ Moved My Body
☐ Expressed Gratitude
☐ Reflected on the day

AFFIRMATION OF THE DAY

REMEMBER

MORNING INTENTIONS

Morning Thoughts Feelings & Intuitions

How do you want to feel today?

What do you want to accomplish today?

EVENING REFLECTIONS

Evening Thoughts Feelings & Intuitions

How did you feel today?

What did you accomplish today?

GRATITUDE LIST

1.

2.

3.

Notes

Every step forward , no matter how small is a step in the right direction

Date:

S / M / T / W / T / F / S

Today's Mood

😣 😟 😐 🙂 😃

Sleep time:_____to_____

Hours slept: _____

Self-care practices accomplished today

- ☐ Set intentions
- ☐ Journaling
- ☐ Meditation

- ☐ Nourishing Foods
- ☐ Mindful Eating
- ☐ Went outside

- ☐ Moved My Body
- ☐ Expressed Gratitude
- ☐ Reflected on the day

AFFIRMATION OF THE DAY	REMEMBER

MORNING INTENTIONS

Morning Thoughts Feelings & Intuitions

How do you want to feel today?

What do you want to accomplish today?

EVENING REFLECTIONS

Evening Thoughts Feelings & Intuitions

How did you feel today?

What did you accomplish today?

GRATITUDE LIST

1.

2.

3.

Notes

Weave some magic today

Date:

S / M / T / W / T / F / S

Today's Mood

☹ ☹ 😐 🙂 😃

Sleep time:_____to_____

Hours slept: _____

Self-care practices accomplished today

☐ Set intentions

☐ Journaling

☐ Meditation

☐ Nourishing Foods

☐ Mindful Eating

☐ Went outside

☐ Moved My Body

☐ Expressed Gratitude

☐ Reflected on the day

AFFIRMATION OF THE DAY

REMEMBER

MORNING INTENTIONS

Morning Thoughts Feelings & Intuitions

How do you want to feel today?

What do you want to accomplish today?

EVENING REFLECTIONS

Evening Thoughts Feelings & Intuitions

How did you feel today?

What did you accomplish today?

GRATITUDE LIST

1.

2.

3.

Notes

Sparkle like a glitterball

Date:

S / M / T / W / T / F / S

Today's Mood

😟 😔 😑 🙂 😃

Sleep time:_____to_____

Hours slept: _____

Self-care practices accomplished today

☐ Set intentions
☐ Journaling
☐ Meditation
☐

☐ Nourishing Foods
☐ Mindful Eating
☐ Went outside
☐

☐ Moved My Body
☐ Expressed Gratitude
☐ Reflected on the day
☐

AFFIRMATION OF THE DAY

REMEMBER

MORNING INTENTIONS

Morning Thoughts Feelings & Intuitions

How do you want to feel today?

What do you want to accomplish today?

EVENING REFLECTIONS

Evening Thoughts Feelings & Intuitions

How did you feel today?

What did you accomplish today?

GRATITUDE LIST

1.

2.

3.

Notes

Self-belief makes anything possible

Date:

S / M / T / W / T / F / S

Today's Mood

☹ ☹ 😐 🙂 😀

Sleep time:_____to_____

Hours slept: _____

Self-care practices accomplished today

☐ Set intentions

☐ Journaling

☐ Meditation

☐ Nourishing Foods

☐ Mindful Eating

☐ Went outside

☐ Moved My Body

☐ Expressed Gratitude

☐ Reflected on the day

AFFIRMATION OF THE DAY

REMEMBER

MORNING INTENTIONS

Morning Thoughts Feelings & Intuitions

How do you want to feel today?

What do you want to accomplish today?

EVENING REFLECTIONS

Evening Thoughts Feelings & Intuitions

How did you feel today?

What did you accomplish today?

GRATITUDE LIST

1.

2.

3.

Notes

Truly living is believing you can, and then taking action on it

Weekly Wins

Date:

S / M / T / W / T / F / S

WHAT FUN THINGS DID YOU DO THIS WEEK?

LIST 3 THINGS YOU LOVE ABOUT YOURSELF

WHAT HAVE YOU LEARNT ABOUT YOURSELF THIS WEEK?

Date:

S / M / T / W / T / F / S

Today's Mood

☹ ☹ 😐 ☺ 😀

Sleep time:_____to_____

Hours slept: _____

Self-care practices accomplished today

☐ Set intentions
☐ Journaling
☐ Meditation

☐ Nourishing Foods
☐ Mindful Eating
☐ Went outside

☐ Moved My Body
☐ Expressed Gratitude
☐ Reflected on the day

AFFIRMATION OF THE DAY

REMEMBER

MORNING INTENTIONS

Morning Thoughts Feelings & Intuitions

How do you want to feel today?

What do you want to accomplish today?

EVENING REFLECTIONS

Evening Thoughts Feelings & Intuitions

How did you feel today?

What did you accomplish today?

GRATITUDE LIST

1.

2.

3.

Notes

Remember how special you are

Date:

S / M / T / W / T / F / S

Today's Mood

☹ 🙁 😐 🙂 😀

Sleep time:_____to_____

Hours slept: _____

Self-care practices accomplished today

☐ Set intentions   ☐ Nourishing Foods   ☐ Moved My Body

☐ Journaling   ☐ Mindful Eating   ☐ Expressed Gratitude

☐ Meditation   ☐ Went outside   ☐ Reflected on the day

AFFIRMATION OF THE DAY

REMEMBER

MORNING INTENTIONS

Morning Thoughts Feelings & Intuitions

How do you want to feel today?

What do you want to accomplish today?

EVENING REFLECTIONS

Evening Thoughts Feelings & Intuitions

How did you feel today?

What did you accomplish today?

GRATITUDE LIST

1.

2.

3.

Notes

Your smile is contagious, do it more :)

Date:
S / M / T / W / T / F / S

Today's Mood
😦 😕 😐 🙂 😄

Sleep time:_____to_____

Hours slept: _____

Self-care practices accomplished today

☐ Set intentions
☐ Journaling
☐ Meditation
☐

☐ Nourishing Foods
☐ Mindful Eating
☐ Went outside
☐

☐ Moved My Body
☐ Expressed Gratitude
☐ Reflected on the day
☐

AFFIRMATION OF THE DAY

REMEMBER

MORNING INTENTIONS

Morning Thoughts Feelings & Intuitions

How do you want to feel today?

What do you want to accomplish today?

EVENING REFLECTIONS

Evening Thoughts Feelings & Intuitions

How did you feel today?

What did you accomplish today?

GRATITUDE LIST

1.

2.

3.

Notes

Kindness ripples out like waves on the ocean

Date:

S / M / T / W / T / F / S

Today's Mood

😞 😟 😐 🙂 😀

Sleep time:_____to_____

Hours slept: _____

Self-care practices accomplished today

- ☐ Set intentions
- ☐ Journaling
- ☐ Meditation

- ☐ Nourishing Foods
- ☐ Mindful Eating
- ☐ Went outside

- ☐ Moved My Body
- ☐ Expressed Gratitude
- ☐ Reflected on the day

AFFIRMATION OF THE DAY	REMEMBER

MORNING INTENTIONS

Morning Thoughts Feelings & Intuitions

How do you want to feel today?

What do you want to accomplish today?

EVENING REFLECTIONS

Evening Thoughts Feelings & Intuitions

How did you feel today?

What did you accomplish today?

GRATITUDE LIST

1.

2.

3.

Notes

Go with the flow and you'll learn to ride the waves

Date:

S / M / T / W / T / F / S

Today's Mood

☹ ☹ 😐 🙂 😀

Sleep time:_____to_____

Hours slept: _____

Self-care practices accomplished today

☐ Set intentions
☐ Journaling
☐ Meditation
☐

☐ Nourishing Foods
☐ Mindful Eating
☐ Went outside
☐

☐ Moved My Body
☐ Expressed Gratitude
☐ Reflected on the day
☐

AFFIRMATION OF THE DAY

REMEMBER

MORNING INTENTIONS

Morning Thoughts Feelings & Intuitions

How do you want to feel today?

What do you want to accomplish today?

EVENING REFLECTIONS

Evening Thoughts Feelings & Intuitions

How did you feel today?

What did you accomplish today?

GRATITUDE LIST

1.

2.

3.

Notes

Do something to make you laugh. Embrace your inner child and stress will start to melt away

Date:

S / M / T / W / T / F / S

Today's Mood

☹ ☹ 😐 🙂 😃

Sleep time:_____to_____

Hours slept: _____

Self-care practices accomplished today

☐ Set intentions

☐ Journaling

☐ Meditation

☐ Nourishing Foods

☐ Mindful Eating

☐ Went outside

☐ Moved My Body

☐ Expressed Gratitude

☐ Reflected on the day

AFFIRMATION OF THE DAY	REMEMBER

MORNING INTENTIONS

Morning Thoughts Feelings & Intuitions

How do you want to feel today?

What do you want to accomplish today?

EVENING REFLECTIONS

Evening Thoughts Feelings & Intuitions

How did you feel today?

What did you accomplish today?

GRATITUDE LIST

1.

2.

3.

Notes

You were born to be fabulous

Date:

S / M / T / W / T / F / S

Today's Mood

😣 😔 😐 🙂 😄

Sleep time:_____to_____

Hours slept: _____

Self-care practices accomplished today

☐ Set intentions

☐ Journaling

☐ Meditation

☐

☐ Nourishing Foods

☐ Mindful Eating

☐ Went outside

☐ Moved My Body

☐ Expressed Gratitude

☐ Reflected on the day

☐

AFFIRMATION OF THE DAY

REMEMBER

MORNING INTENTIONS

Morning Thoughts Feelings & Intuitions

How do you want to feel today?

What do you want to accomplish today?

EVENING REFLECTIONS

Evening Thoughts Feelings & Intuitions

How did you feel today?

What did you accomplish today?

GRATITUDE LIST

1.

2.

3.

Notes

Don't try to be anyone else, you are perfectly you

Weekly Wins

Date:

S / M / T / W / T / F / S

WHAT CHALLENGES DID YOU OVERCOME THIS WEEK?

HOW HAVE YOU BEEN KIND TO YOURSELF THIS WEEK?

WHAT CAN YOU RELEASE THAT YOU NO LONGER NEED?

Date:

S / M / T / W / T / F / S

Today's Mood

☹ ☹ 😐 ☺ 😀

Sleep time:_____to_____

Hours slept: _____

Self-care practices accomplished today

☐ Set intentions
☐ Journaling
☐ Meditation

☐ Nourishing Foods
☐ Mindful Eating
☐ Went outside

☐ Moved My Body
☐ Expressed Gratitude
☐ Reflected on the day

AFFIRMATION OF THE DAY

REMEMBER

MORNING INTENTIONS

Morning Thoughts Feelings & Intuitions

How do you want to feel today?

What do you want to accomplish today?

EVENING REFLECTIONS

Evening Thoughts Feelings & Intuitions

How did you feel today?

What did you accomplish today?

GRATITUDE LIST

1.

2.

3.

Notes

Treat yourself, you deserve it

Date:

S / M / T / W / T / F / S

Today's Mood

☹ ☹ 😐 ☺ 😃

Sleep time:_____to_____

Hours slept: _____

Self-care practices accomplished today

- [ ] Set intentions
- [ ] Journaling
- [ ] Meditation

- [ ] Nourishing Foods
- [ ] Mindful Eating
- [ ] Went outside

- [ ] Moved My Body
- [ ] Expressed Gratitude
- [ ] Reflected on the day

AFFIRMATION OF THE DAY

REMEMBER

MORNING INTENTIONS

Morning Thoughts Feelings & Intuitions

How do you want to feel today?

What do you want to accomplish today?

EVENING REFLECTIONS

Evening Thoughts Feelings & Intuitions

How did you feel today?

What did you accomplish today?

GRATITUDE LIST

1.

2.

3.

Notes

Go sprinkle your glitter wherever you go

Date:

S / M / T / W / T / F / S

Today's Mood

☹ ☹ 😐 🙂 😀

Sleep time:_____to_____

Hours slept: _____

Self-care practices accomplished today

☐ Set intentions
☐ Journaling
☐ Meditation
☐

☐ Nourishing Foods
☐ Mindful Eating
☐ Went outside
☐

☐ Moved My Body
☐ Expressed Gratitude
☐ Reflected on the day
☐

AFFIRMATION OF THE DAY

REMEMBER

MORNING INTENTIONS

Morning Thoughts Feelings & Intuitions

How do you want to feel today?

What do you want to accomplish today?

EVENING REFLECTIONS

Evening Thoughts Feelings & Intuitions

How did you feel today?

What did you accomplish today?

GRATITUDE LIST

1.

2.

3.

Notes

Did you remember how amazing you are today?

Date:

S / M / T / W / T / F / S

Today's Mood

😫 😟 😐 🙂 😃

Sleep time:_____to_____

Hours slept: _____

Self-care practices accomplished today

- ☐ Set intentions
- ☐ Journaling
- ☐ Meditation

- ☐ Nourishing Foods
- ☐ Mindful Eating
- ☐ Went outside

- ☐ Moved My Body
- ☐ Expressed Gratitude
- ☐ Reflected on the day

AFFIRMATION OF THE DAY

REMEMBER

MORNING INTENTIONS

Morning Thoughts Feelings & Intuitions

How do you want to feel today?

What do you want to accomplish today?

EVENING REFLECTIONS

Evening Thoughts Feelings & Intuitions

How did you feel today?

What did you accomplish today?

GRATITUDE LIST

1.

2.

3.

Notes

Take a moment out and take some slow, mindful breaths

Date:

S / M / T / W / T / F / S

Today's Mood

☹ ☹ 😐 ☺ 😃

Sleep time:_____to_____

Hours slept: _____

Self-care practices accomplished today

☐	Set intentions
☐	Journaling
☐	Meditation
☐	

☐	Nourishing Foods
☐	Mindful Eating
☐	Went outside
☐	

☐	Moved My Body
☐	Expressed Gratitude
☐	Reflected on the day
☐	

AFFIRMATION OF THE DAY

REMEMBER

MORNING INTENTIONS

Morning Thoughts Feelings & Intuitions

How do you want to feel today?

What do you want to accomplish today?

EVENING REFLECTIONS

Evening Thoughts Feelings & Intuitions

How did you feel today?

What did you accomplish today?

GRATITUDE LIST

1.

2.

3.

Notes

You are fearlessly fabulous

Date:

S / M / T / W / T / F / S

Today's Mood

☹ ☹ 😐 🙂 😀

Sleep time:_____to_____

Hours slept: _____

Self-care practices accomplished today

☐ Set intentions

☐ Journaling

☐ Meditation

☐ _____

☐ Nourishing Foods

☐ Mindful Eating

☐ Went outside

☐ _____

☐ Moved My Body

☐ Expressed Gratitude

☐ Reflected on the day

☐ _____

AFFIRMATION OF THE DAY

REMEMBER

MORNING INTENTIONS

Morning Thoughts Feelings & Intuitions

How do you want to feel today?

What do you want to accomplish today?

EVENING REFLECTIONS

Evening Thoughts Feelings & Intuitions

How did you feel today?

What did you accomplish today?

GRATITUDE LIST

1.

2.

3.

Notes ♥

Dip your toe into something new, you might just love it!

Date:

S / M / T / W / T / F / S

Today's Mood 😣 😞 😐 🙂 😃

Sleep time:_____to_____

Hours slept: _____

Self-care practices accomplished today

☐ Set intentions
☐ Journaling
☐ Meditation

☐ Nourishing Foods
☐ Mindful Eating
☐ Went outside

☐ Moved My Body
☐ Expressed Gratitude
☐ Reflected on the day

AFFIRMATION OF THE DAY

REMEMBER

MORNING INTENTIONS

Morning Thoughts Feelings & Intuitions

How do you want to feel today?

What do you want to accomplish today?

EVENING REFLECTIONS

Evening Thoughts Feelings & Intuitions

How did you feel today?

What did you accomplish today?

GRATITUDE LIST

1.

2.

3.

Notes

Unleash your kindness into the world

Weekly Wins

Date:

S / M / T / W / T / F / S

WHAT ARE YOUR TAKEAWAY THOUGHTS FROM LAST WEEK?

WHAT DID YOU DO TO LAUGH?

LIST 3 THINGS YOU'RE PROUD OF FROM LAST WEEK

Date:

S / M / T / W / T / F / S

Today's Mood

☹ ☹ 😐 🙂 😀

Sleep time:_____to_____

Hours slept: _____

Self-care practices accomplished today

☐ Set intentions

☐ Journaling

☐ Meditation

☐ Nourishing Foods

☐ Mindful Eating

☐ Went outside

☐ Moved My Body

☐ Expressed Gratitude

☐ Reflected on the day

AFFIRMATION OF THE DAY

REMEMBER

MORNING INTENTIONS

Morning Thoughts Feelings & Intuitions

How do you want to feel today?

What do you want to accomplish today?

EVENING REFLECTIONS

Evening Thoughts Feelings & Intuitions

How did you feel today?

What did you accomplish today?

GRATITUDE LIST

1.

2.

3.

Notes

Empower others and you too will be empowered

Date:

S / M / T / W / T / F / S

Today's Mood

☹ ☹ 😐 🙂 😃

Sleep time:_____to_____

Hours slept: _____

Self-care practices accomplished today

- [ ] Set intentions
- [ ] Journaling
- [ ] Meditation
- [ ]

- [ ] Nourishing Foods
- [ ] Mindful Eating
- [ ] Went outside
- [ ]

- [ ] Moved My Body
- [ ] Expressed Gratitude
- [ ] Reflected on the day
- [ ]

AFFIRMATION OF THE DAY

REMEMBER

MORNING INTENTIONS

Morning Thoughts Feelings & Intuitions

How do you want to feel today?

What do you want to accomplish today?

EVENING REFLECTIONS

Evening Thoughts Feelings & Intuitions

How did you feel today?

What did you accomplish today?

GRATITUDE LIST

1.

2.

3.

Notes

You can make your daydream a reality

Date:

S / M / T / W / T / F / S

Today's Mood

😖 😟 😐 🙂 😃

Sleep time:_____to_____

Hours slept: _____

Self-care practices accomplished today

☐	Set intentions
☐	Journaling
☐	Meditation
☐	

☐	Nourishing Foods
☐	Mindful Eating
☐	Went outside
☐	

☐	Moved My Body
☐	Expressed Gratitude
☐	Reflected on the day
☐	

AFFIRMATION OF THE DAY

REMEMBER

MORNING INTENTIONS

Morning Thoughts Feelings & Intuitions

How do you want to feel today?

What do you want to accomplish today?

EVENING REFLECTIONS

Evening Thoughts Feelings & Intuitions

How did you feel today?

What did you accomplish today?

GRATITUDE LIST

1.

2.

3.

Notes

Share your uniqueness with the world

Date: Today's Mood

S / M / T / W / T / F / S   🙁 😟 😐 🙂 😄

Sleep time:_____to_____

Hours slept: _____

Self-care practices accomplished today

- [ ] Set intentions
- [ ] Journaling
- [ ] Meditation
- [ ]

- [ ] Nourishing Foods
- [ ] Mindful Eating
- [ ] Went outside

- [ ] Moved My Body
- [ ] Expressed Gratitude
- [ ] Reflected on the day

AFFIRMATION OF THE DAY

REMEMBER

MORNING INTENTIONS

Morning Thoughts Feelings & Intuitions

How do you want to feel today?

What do you want to accomplish today?

EVENING REFLECTIONS

Evening Thoughts Feelings & Intuitions

How did you feel today?

What did you accomplish today?

GRATITUDE LIST

1.

2.

3.

Notes

Stop believing you can't and remember that you can

Date:

S / M / T / W / T / F / S

Today's Mood ☹ ☹ 😐 🙂 😀

Sleep time:_____to_____

Hours slept: _____

Self-care practices accomplished today

☐ Set intentions	☐ Nourishing Foods	☐ Moved My Body
☐ Journaling	☐ Mindful Eating	☐ Expressed Gratitude
☐ Meditation	☐ Went outside	☐ Reflected on the day
☐	☐	☐

AFFIRMATION OF THE DAY

REMEMBER

MORNING INTENTIONS

Morning Thoughts Feelings & Intuitions

How do you want to feel today?

What do you want to accomplish today?

EVENING REFLECTIONS

Evening Thoughts Feelings & Intuitions

How did you feel today?

What did you accomplish today?

GRATITUDE LIST

1.

2.

3.

Notes

A happier you is just around the corner. You can find her by being kind to yourself now

Date:

S / M / T / W / T / F / S

Today's Mood

☹ 😞 😐 🙂 😃

Sleep time:_____to_____

Hours slept: _____

Self-care practices accomplished today

☐ Set intentions

☐ Journaling

☐ Meditation

☐

☐ Nourishing Foods

☐ Mindful Eating

☐ Went outside

☐

☐ Moved My Body

☐ Expressed Gratitude

☐ Reflected on the day

☐

AFFIRMATION OF THE DAY	REMEMBER

MORNING INTENTIONS

Morning Thoughts Feelings & Intuitions

How do you want to feel today?

What do you want to accomplish today?

EVENING REFLECTIONS

Evening Thoughts Feelings & Intuitions

How did you feel today?

What did you accomplish today?

GRATITUDE LIST

1.

2.

3.

Notes

What are you waiting for? Go grab the life you want now

Date:

S / M / T / W / T / F / S

Today's Mood

☹ ☹ 😐 🙂 😃

Sleep time:_____to_____

Hours slept: _____

Self-care practices accomplished today

☐ Set intentions

☐ Journaling

☐ Meditation

☐ Nourishing Foods

☐ Mindful Eating

☐ Went outside

☐ Moved My Body

☐ Expressed Gratitude

☐ Reflected on the day

AFFIRMATION OF THE DAY

REMEMBER

MORNING INTENTIONS

Morning Thoughts Feelings & Intuitions

How do you want to feel today?

What do you want to accomplish today?

EVENING REFLECTIONS

Evening Thoughts Feelings & Intuitions

How did you feel today?

What did you accomplish today?

GRATITUDE LIST

1.

2.

3.

Notes

You deserve the best, believe it!

Weekly Wins

Date:

S / M / T / W / T / F / S

WHAT WERE THE BEST MOMENTS OF THE WEEK?

GIVE YOURSELF A COMPLIMENT

WHAT SELF-CARE PRACTICES DID YOU LOVE DOING THIS WEEK?

Date:

S / M / T / W / T / F / S

Today's Mood

☹ ☹ 😐 🙂 😃

Sleep time:_____to_____

Hours slept: _____

Self-care practices accomplished today

☐ Set intentions
☐ Journaling
☐ Meditation

☐ Nourishing Foods
☐ Mindful Eating
☐ Went outside

☐ Moved My Body
☐ Expressed Gratitude
☐ Reflected on the day

AFFIRMATION OF THE DAY

REMEMBER

MORNING INTENTIONS

Morning Thoughts Feelings & Intuitions

How do you want to feel today?

What do you want to accomplish today?

EVENING REFLECTIONS

Evening Thoughts Feelings & Intuitions

How did you feel today?

What did you accomplish today?

GRATITUDE LIST

1.

2.

3.

Notes

Relax, there's nowhere you have to be, other than in this moment

Date:

S / M / T / W / T / F / S

Today's Mood

😣 😟 😐 🙂 😄

Sleep time:_____to_____

Hours slept: _____

Self-care practices accomplished today

- [ ] Set intentions
- [ ] Journaling
- [ ] Meditation

- [ ] Nourishing Foods
- [ ] Mindful Eating
- [ ] Went outside

- [ ] Moved My Body
- [ ] Expressed Gratitude
- [ ] Reflected on the day

AFFIRMATION OF THE DAY

REMEMBER

MORNING INTENTIONS

Morning Thoughts Feelings & Intuitions

How do you want to feel today?

What do you want to accomplish today?

EVENING REFLECTIONS

Evening Thoughts Feelings & Intuitions

How did you feel today?

What did you accomplish today?

GRATITUDE LIST

1.

2.

3.

Notes

Don't pay attention to what others think of you......the only relevant opinion is yours.

Date:

S / M / T / W / T / F / S

Today's Mood

☹ ☹ 😐 🙂 😃

Sleep time:_____to_____

Hours slept: _____

Self-care practices accomplished today

☐ Set intentions

☐ Journaling

☐ Meditation

☐ Nourishing Foods

☐ Mindful Eating

☐ Went outside

☐ Moved My Body

☐ Expressed Gratitude

☐ Reflected on the day

AFFIRMATION OF THE DAY

REMEMBER

MORNING INTENTIONS

Morning Thoughts Feelings & Intuitions

How do you want to feel today?

What do you want to accomplish today?

EVENING REFLECTIONS

Evening Thoughts Feelings & Intuitions

How did you feel today?

What did you accomplish today?

GRATITUDE LIST

1.

2.

3.

Notes

Say something kind to yourself right now.....and mean it

Date:

S / M / T / W / T / F / S

Today's Mood

☹ ☹ 😐 🙂 😃

Sleep time:_____to_____

Hours slept: _____

Self-care practices accomplished today

☐ Set intentions

☐ Journaling

☐ Meditation

☐ Nourishing Foods

☐ Mindful Eating

☐ Went outside

☐ Moved My Body

☐ Expressed Gratitude

☐ Reflected on the day

AFFIRMATION OF THE DAY

REMEMBER

MORNING INTENTIONS

Morning Thoughts Feelings & Intuitions

How do you want to feel today?

What do you want to accomplish today?

EVENING REFLECTIONS

Evening Thoughts Feelings & Intuitions

How did you feel today?

What did you accomplish today?

GRATITUDE LIST

1.

2.

3.

Notes

Put your hand over your heart and take a moment to relax right now

Date:

S / M / T / W / T / F / S

Today's Mood

☹ ☹ 😐 🙂 😃

Sleep time:_____to_____

Hours slept: _____

Self-care practices accomplished today

☐ Set intentions

☐ Journaling

☐ Meditation

☐ Nourishing Foods

☐ Mindful Eating

☐ Went outside

☐ Moved My Body

☐ Expressed Gratitude

☐ Reflected on the day

AFFIRMATION OF THE DAY

REMEMBER

MORNING INTENTIONS

Morning Thoughts Feelings & Intuitions

How do you want to feel today?

What do you want to accomplish today?

EVENING REFLECTIONS

Evening Thoughts Feelings & Intuitions

How did you feel today?

What did you accomplish today?

GRATITUDE LIST

1.

2.

3.

Notes

You are a bright star. Go shine your light and guide the way

Date:

S / M / T / W / T / F / S

Today's Mood

☹ ☹ 😐 🙂 😀

Sleep time:_____to_____

Hours slept: _____

Self-care practices accomplished today

☐ Set intentions
☐ Journaling
☐ Meditation

☐ Nourishing Foods
☐ Mindful Eating
☐ Went outside

☐ Moved My Body
☐ Expressed Gratitude
☐ Reflected on the day

AFFIRMATION OF THE DAY

REMEMBER

MORNING INTENTIONS

Morning Thoughts Feelings & Intuitions

How do you want to feel today?

What do you want to accomplish today?

EVENING REFLECTIONS

Evening Thoughts Feelings & Intuitions

How did you feel today?

What did you accomplish today?

GRATITUDE LIST

1.

2.

3.

Notes

Be gentle on yourself

Date:

S / M / T / W / T / F / S

Today's Mood

☹ ☹ 😐 ☺ 😃

Sleep time:_____to_____

Hours slept: _____

Self-care practices accomplished today

☐ Set intentions	☐ Nourishing Foods	☐ Moved My Body
☐ Journaling	☐ Mindful Eating	☐ Expressed Gratitude
☐ Meditation	☐ Went outside	☐ Reflected on the day

AFFIRMATION OF THE DAY

REMEMBER

MORNING INTENTIONS

Morning Thoughts Feelings & Intuitions

How do you want to feel today?

What do you want to accomplish today?

EVENING REFLECTIONS

Evening Thoughts Feelings & Intuitions

How did you feel today?

What did you accomplish today?

GRATITUDE LIST

1.

2.

3.

Notes

Life is not a race. Enjoy the journey, take time out to explore new avenues on the way

Weekly Wins

Date:

S / M / T / W / T / F / S

WHAT FUN THINGS DID YOU DO THIS WEEK?

LIST 3 THINGS YOU LOVE ABOUT YOURSELF

WHAT HAVE YOU LEARNT ABOUT YOURSELF THIS WEEK?

Date:

S / M / T / W / T / F / S

Today's Mood ☹ ☹ 😐 🙂 😁

Sleep time:_____to_____

Hours slept: _____

Self-care practices accomplished today

☐ Set intentions
☐ Journaling
☐ Meditation

☐ Nourishing Foods
☐ Mindful Eating
☐ Went outside

☐ Moved My Body
☐ Expressed Gratitude
☐ Reflected on the day

AFFIRMATION OF THE DAY

REMEMBER

MORNING INTENTIONS

Morning Thoughts Feelings & Intuitions

How do you want to feel today?

What do you want to accomplish today?

EVENING REFLECTIONS

Evening Thoughts Feelings & Intuitions

How did you feel today?

What did you accomplish today?

GRATITUDE LIST

1.

2.

3.

Notes

Believe in yourself as much as you believe in others

Date:

S / M / T / W / T / F / S

Today's Mood

☹ ☹ 😐 🙂 😃

Sleep time:_____to_____

Hours slept: _____

Self-care practices accomplished today

☐ Set intentions
☐ Journaling
☐ Meditation

☐ Nourishing Foods
☐ Mindful Eating
☐ Went outside

☐ Moved My Body
☐ Expressed Gratitude
☐ Reflected on the day

AFFIRMATION OF THE DAY

REMEMBER

MORNING INTENTIONS

Morning Thoughts Feelings & Intuitions

How do you want to feel today?

What do you want to accomplish today?

EVENING REFLECTIONS

Evening Thoughts Feelings & Intuitions

How did you feel today?

What did you accomplish today?

GRATITUDE LIST

1.

2.

3.

Notes

Keep going, you're doing amazingly

Date:

S / M / T / W / T / F / S

Today's Mood

☹ ☹ 😐 ☺ 😄

Sleep time:_____to_____

Hours slept: _____

Self-care practices accomplished today

- ☐ Set intentions
- ☐ Journaling
- ☐ Meditation
- ☐

- ☐ Nourishing Foods
- ☐ Mindful Eating
- ☐ Went outside
- ☐

- ☐ Moved My Body
- ☐ Expressed Gratitude
- ☐ Reflected on the day
- ☐

AFFIRMATION OF THE DAY

REMEMBER

MORNING INTENTIONS

Morning Thoughts Feelings & Intuitions

How do you want to feel today?

What do you want to accomplish today?

EVENING REFLECTIONS

Evening Thoughts Feelings & Intuitions

How did you feel today?

What did you accomplish today?

GRATITUDE LIST

1.

2.

3.

Notes

Forgive yourself for your past mistakes. Holding on only holds you back

Date:

S / M / T / W / T / F / S

Today's Mood

😫 😣 😐 🙂 😃

Sleep time:_____to_____

Hours slept: _____

Self-care practices accomplished today

- [ ] Set intentions
- [ ] Journaling
- [ ] Meditation

- [ ] Nourishing Foods
- [ ] Mindful Eating
- [ ] Went outside

- [ ] Moved My Body
- [ ] Expressed Gratitude
- [ ] Reflected on the day

AFFIRMATION OF THE DAY

REMEMBER

MORNING INTENTIONS

Morning Thoughts Feelings & Intuitions

How do you want to feel today?

What do you want to accomplish today?

EVENING REFLECTIONS

Evening Thoughts Feelings & Intuitions

How did you feel today?

What did you accomplish today?

GRATITUDE LIST

1.

2.

3.

Notes

You are more magical than you dare to believe

Date:

S / M / T / W / T / F / S

Today's Mood

☹ ☹ 😐 🙂 😄

Sleep time:_____to_____

Hours slept: _____

Self-care practices accomplished today

- ☐ Set intentions
- ☐ Journaling
- ☐ Meditation
- ☐

- ☐ Nourishing Foods
- ☐ Mindful Eating
- ☐ Went outside

- ☐ Moved My Body
- ☐ Expressed Gratitude
- ☐ Reflected on the day

AFFIRMATION OF THE DAY

REMEMBER

MORNING INTENTIONS

Morning Thoughts Feelings & Intuitions

How do you want to feel today?

What do you want to accomplish today?

EVENING REFLECTIONS

Evening Thoughts Feelings & Intuitions

How did you feel today?

What did you accomplish today?

GRATITUDE LIST

1.

2.

3.

Notes

Believe you can and you will

Date:

S / M / T / W / T / F / S

Today's Mood

☹ ☹ 😐 🙂 😃

Sleep time:_____to_____

Hours slept: _____

Self-care practices accomplished today

- [ ] Set intentions
- [ ] Journaling
- [ ] Meditation

- [ ] Nourishing Foods
- [ ] Mindful Eating
- [ ] Went outside

- [ ] Moved My Body
- [ ] Expressed Gratitude
- [ ] Reflected on the day

AFFIRMATION OF THE DAY

REMEMBER

MORNING INTENTIONS

Morning Thoughts Feelings & Intuitions

How do you want to feel today?

What do you want to accomplish today?

EVENING REFLECTIONS

Evening Thoughts Feelings & Intuitions

How did you feel today?

What did you accomplish today?

GRATITUDE LIST

1.

2.

3.

Notes

Don't talk to yourself in ways that you would never talk to anyone else

Date:
S / M / T / W / T / F / S

Today's Mood
😣 😟 😐 🙂 😃

Sleep time:_____to_____

Hours slept: _____

Self-care practices accomplished today

- Set intentions
- Journaling
- Meditation

- Nourishing Foods
- Mindful Eating
- Went outside

- Moved My Body
- Expressed Gratitude
- Reflected on the day

AFFIRMATION OF THE DAY

REMEMBER

MORNING INTENTIONS

Morning Thoughts Feelings & Intuitions

How do you want to feel today?

What do you want to accomplish today?

EVENING REFLECTIONS

Evening Thoughts Feelings & Intuitions

How did you feel today?

What did you accomplish today?

GRATITUDE LIST

1.

2.

3.

Notes

Time for an adventure?

Weekly Wins

Date:

S / M / T / W / T / F / S

WHAT CHALLENGES DID YOU OVERCOME THIS WEEK?

HOW HAVE YOU BEEN KIND TO YOURSELF THIS WEEK?

WHAT CAN YOU RELEASE THAT YOU NO LONGER NEED?

Date:

S / M / T / W / T / F / S

Today's Mood

☹ ☹ 😐 🙂 😃

Sleep time:_____to_____

Hours slept: _____

Self-care practices accomplished today

- [ ] Set intentions
- [ ] Journaling
- [ ] Meditation

- [ ] Nourishing Foods
- [ ] Mindful Eating
- [ ] Went outside

- [ ] Moved My Body
- [ ] Expressed Gratitude
- [ ] Reflected on the day

AFFIRMATION OF THE DAY

REMEMBER

MORNING INTENTIONS

Morning Thoughts Feelings & Intuitions

How do you want to feel today?

What do you want to accomplish today?

EVENING REFLECTIONS

Evening Thoughts Feelings & Intuitions

How did you feel today?

What did you accomplish today?

GRATITUDE LIST

1.

2.

3.

Notes

Your feelings matter

Date:

S / M / T / W / T / F / S

Today's Mood

☹ ☹ 😐 🙂 😃

Sleep time:_____to_____

Hours slept: _____

Self-care practices accomplished today

☐ Set intentions

☐ Journaling

☐ Meditation

☐ Nourishing Foods

☐ Mindful Eating

☐ Went outside

☐ Moved My Body

☐ Expressed Gratitude

☐ Reflected on the day

AFFIRMATION OF THE DAY

REMEMBER

MORNING INTENTIONS

Morning Thoughts Feelings & Intuitions

How do you want to feel today?

What do you want to accomplish today?

EVENING REFLECTIONS

Evening Thoughts Feelings & Intuitions

How did you feel today?

What did you accomplish today?

GRATITUDE LIST

1.

2.

3.

Notes

Shine like a lighthouse in the dark

Date:

S / M / T / W / T / F / S

Today's Mood

☹ ☹ 😐 ☺ 😄

Sleep time:_____to_____

Hours slept: _____

Self-care practices accomplished today

☐ Set intentions
☐ Journaling
☐ Meditation
☐

☐ Nourishing Foods
☐ Mindful Eating
☐ Went outside
☐

☐ Moved My Body
☐ Expressed Gratitude
☐ Reflected on the day
☐

AFFIRMATION OF THE DAY

REMEMBER

MORNING INTENTIONS

Morning Thoughts Feelings & Intuitions

How do you want to feel today?

What do you want to accomplish today?

EVENING REFLECTIONS

Evening Thoughts Feelings & Intuitions

How did you feel today?

What did you accomplish today?

GRATITUDE LIST

1.

2.

3.

Notes

You write the next chapter of your life, what's the plot?

Date:

S / M / T / W / T / F / S

Today's Mood

☹ 😦 😐 🙂 😃

Sleep time:_____to_____

Hours slept: _____

Self-care practices accomplished today

☐ Set intentions
☐ Journaling
☐ Meditation

☐ Nourishing Foods
☐ Mindful Eating
☐ Went outside

☐ Moved My Body
☐ Expressed Gratitude
☐ Reflected on the day

AFFIRMATION OF THE DAY

REMEMBER

MORNING INTENTIONS

Morning Thoughts Feelings & Intuitions

How do you want to feel today?

What do you want to accomplish today?

EVENING REFLECTIONS

Evening Thoughts Feelings & Intuitions

How did you feel today?

What did you accomplish today?

GRATITUDE LIST

1.

2.

3.

Notes

You are and you will always be the answer

Date:

S / M / T / W / T / F / S

Today's Mood

🙁 😟 😐 🙂 😃

Sleep time:_____to_____

Hours slept: _____

Self-care practices accomplished today

☐ Set intentions
☐ Journaling
☐ Meditation
☐

☐ Nourishing Foods
☐ Mindful Eating
☐ Went outside
☐

☐ Moved My Body
☐ Expressed Gratitude
☐ Reflected on the day
☐

AFFIRMATION OF THE DAY

REMEMBER

MORNING INTENTIONS

Morning Thoughts Feelings & Intuitions

How do you want to feel today?

What do you want to accomplish today?

EVENING REFLECTIONS

Evening Thoughts Feelings & Intuitions

How did you feel today?

What did you accomplish today?

GRATITUDE LIST

1.

2.

3.

Notes

Remember that you are a beautiful soul inside and out

Date:

S / M / T / W / T / F / S

Today's Mood

☹ ☹ 😐 🙂 😄

Sleep time:_____to_____

Hours slept: _____

Self-care practices accomplished today

☐ Set intentions

☐ Journaling

☐ Meditation

☐ Nourishing Foods

☐ Mindful Eating

☐ Went outside

☐ Moved My Body

☐ Expressed Gratitude

☐ Reflected on the day

AFFIRMATION OF THE DAY

REMEMBER

MORNING INTENTIONS

Morning Thoughts Feelings & Intuitions

How do you want to feel today?

What do you want to accomplish today?

EVENING REFLECTIONS

Evening Thoughts Feelings & Intuitions

How did you feel today?

What did you accomplish today?

GRATITUDE LIST

1.

2.

3.

Notes

Today I will say yes to me!

Date:

S / M / T / W / T / F / S

Today's Mood

🙁 😟 😐 🙂 😃

Sleep time:_____to_____

Hours slept: _____

Self-care practices accomplished today

- ☐ Set intentions
- ☐ Journaling
- ☐ Meditation

- ☐ Nourishing Foods
- ☐ Mindful Eating
- ☐ Went outside

- ☐ Moved My Body
- ☐ Expressed Gratitude
- ☐ Reflected on the day

AFFIRMATION OF THE DAY	REMEMBER

MORNING INTENTIONS

Morning Thoughts Feelings & Intuitions

How do you want to feel today?

What do you want to accomplish today?

EVENING REFLECTIONS

Evening Thoughts Feelings & Intuitions

How did you feel today?

What did you accomplish today?

GRATITUDE LIST

1.

2.

3.

Notes

Love yourself a little bit more everyday

Weekly Wins

Date:

S / M / T / W / T / F / S

WHAT ARE YOUR TAKEAWAY THOUGHTS FROM LAST WEEK?

WHAT DID YOU DO TO LAUGH?

LIST 3 THINGS YOU'RE PROUD OF FROM LAST WEEK

Date:

S / M / T / W / T / F / S

Today's Mood

☹ ☹ 😐 🙂 😀

Sleep time:_____to_____

Hours slept: _____

Self-care practices accomplished today

☐ Set intentions
☐ Journaling
☐ Meditation

☐ Nourishing Foods
☐ Mindful Eating
☐ Went outside

☐ Moved My Body
☐ Expressed Gratitude
☐ Reflected on the day

AFFIRMATION OF THE DAY

REMEMBER

MORNING INTENTIONS

Morning Thoughts Feelings & Intuitions

How do you want to feel today?

What do you want to accomplish today?

EVENING REFLECTIONS

Evening Thoughts Feelings & Intuitions

How did you feel today?

What did you accomplish today?

GRATITUDE LIST

1.

2.

3.

Notes

One step forward is all it takes to gain momentum...keep going

Date:

S / M / T / W / T / F / S

Today's Mood

☹ ☹ 😐 🙂 😄

Sleep time:_____to_____

Hours slept: _____

Self-care practices accomplished today

☐ Set intentions
☐ Journaling
☐ Meditation

☐ Nourishing Foods
☐ Mindful Eating
☐ Went outside

☐ Moved My Body
☐ Expressed Gratitude
☐ Reflected on the day

AFFIRMATION OF THE DAY	REMEMBER

MORNING INTENTIONS

Morning Thoughts Feelings & Intuitions

How do you want to feel today?

What do you want to accomplish today?

EVENING REFLECTIONS

Evening Thoughts Feelings & Intuitions

How did you feel today?

What did you accomplish today?

GRATITUDE LIST

1.

2.

3.

Notes

Own your awesomeness every single day

Date:

S / M / T / W / T / F / S

Today's Mood

😣 😞 😐 🙂 😃

Sleep time:_____to_____

Hours slept: _____

Self-care practices accomplished today

☐ Set intentions
☐ Journaling
☐ Meditation

☐ Nourishing Foods
☐ Mindful Eating
☐ Went outside

☐ Moved My Body
☐ Expressed Gratitude
☐ Reflected on the day

AFFIRMATION OF THE DAY	REMEMBER

MORNING INTENTIONS

Morning Thoughts Feelings & Intuitions

How do you want to feel today?

What do you want to accomplish today?

EVENING REFLECTIONS

Evening Thoughts Feelings & Intuitions

How did you feel today?

What did you accomplish today?

GRATITUDE LIST

1.

2.

3.

Notes

When you learn to trust your instincts, anything is possible

Date:

S / M / T / W / T / F / S

Today's Mood

☹ ☹ 😐 🙂 😊

Sleep time:_____to_____

Hours slept: _____

Self-care practices accomplished today

☐ Set intentions
☐ Journaling
☐ Meditation

☐ Nourishing Foods
☐ Mindful Eating
☐ Went outside

☐ Moved My Body
☐ Expressed Gratitude
☐ Reflected on the day

AFFIRMATION OF THE DAY

REMEMBER

MORNING INTENTIONS

Morning Thoughts Feelings & Intuitions

How do you want to feel today?

What do you want to accomplish today?

EVENING REFLECTIONS

Evening Thoughts Feelings & Intuitions

How did you feel today?

What did you accomplish today?

GRATITUDE LIST

1.

2.

3.

Notes

Everyone is born a star. It's up to you when you light up the sky

Date:

S / M / T / W / T / F / S

Today's Mood

☹ ☹ 😐 🙂 😃

Sleep time:_____to_____

Hours slept: _____

Self-care practices accomplished today

- [ ] Set intentions
- [ ] Journaling
- [ ] Meditation

- [ ] Nourishing Foods
- [ ] Mindful Eating
- [ ] Went outside

- [ ] Moved My Body
- [ ] Expressed Gratitude
- [ ] Reflected on the day

AFFIRMATION OF THE DAY

REMEMBER

MORNING INTENTIONS

Morning Thoughts Feelings & Intuitions

How do you want to feel today?

What do you want to accomplish today?

EVENING REFLECTIONS

Evening Thoughts Feelings & Intuitions

How did you feel today?

What did you accomplish today?

GRATITUDE LIST

1.

2.

3.

Notes

Why are you holding off on your dream? Dreams can become reality if you believe

Date:
S / M / T / W / T / F / S

Today's Mood
☹ ☹ 😐 🙂 😄

Sleep time:_____to_____

Hours slept: _____

Self-care practices accomplished today

☐ Set intentions
☐ Journaling
☐ Meditation
☐

☐ Nourishing Foods
☐ Mindful Eating
☐ Went outside
☐

☐ Moved My Body
☐ Expressed Gratitude
☐ Reflected on the day
☐

AFFIRMATION OF THE DAY

REMEMBER

MORNING INTENTIONS

Morning Thoughts Feelings & Intuitions

How do you want to feel today?

What do you want to accomplish today?

EVENING REFLECTIONS

Evening Thoughts Feelings & Intuitions

How did you feel today?

What did you accomplish today?

GRATITUDE LIST

1.

2.

3.

Notes

Look for subtle clues around you that you are heading in the right direction. The universe will guide and support you

Date:

S / M / T / W / T / F / S

Today's Mood

☹ ☹ 😐 🙂 😃

Sleep time:_____to_____

Hours slept: _____

Self-care practices accomplished today

☐ Set intentions
☐ Journaling
☐ Meditation

☐ Nourishing Foods
☐ Mindful Eating
☐ Went outside

☐ Moved My Body
☐ Expressed Gratitude
☐ Reflected on the day

AFFIRMATION OF THE DAY

REMEMBER

MORNING INTENTIONS

Morning Thoughts Feelings & Intuitions

How do you want to feel today?

What do you want to accomplish today?

EVENING REFLECTIONS

Evening Thoughts Feelings & Intuitions

How did you feel today?

What did you accomplish today?

GRATITUDE LIST

1.

2.

3.

Notes

Take a moment right here, right now to breathe deeply. With your exhale let it all go

Weekly Wins

Date:

S / M / T / W / T / F / S

WHAT WERE THE BEST MOMENTS OF THE WEEK?

GIVE YOURSELF A COMPLIMENT

WHAT SELF-CARE PRACTICES DID YOU LOVE DOING THIS WEEK?

Date:

S / M / T / W / T / F / S

Today's Mood

☹ ☹ 😐 🙂 😁

Sleep time:_____to_____

Hours slept: _____

Self-care practices accomplished today

- [ ] Set intentions
- [ ] Journaling
- [ ] Meditation
- [ ]

- [ ] Nourishing Foods
- [ ] Mindful Eating
- [ ] Went outside
- [ ]

- [ ] Moved My Body
- [ ] Expressed Gratitude
- [ ] Reflected on the day
- [ ]

AFFIRMATION OF THE DAY

REMEMBER

MORNING INTENTIONS

Morning Thoughts Feelings & Intuitions

How do you want to feel today?

What do you want to accomplish today?

EVENING REFLECTIONS

Evening Thoughts Feelings & Intuitions

How did you feel today?

What did you accomplish today?

GRATITUDE LIST

1.

2.

3.

Notes

Anything is possible, trust your intuition

Date:

S / M / T / W / T / F / S

Today's Mood

😞 😟 😐 🙂 😃

Sleep time:_____to_____

Hours slept: _____

Self-care practices accomplished today

- ☐ Set intentions
- ☐ Journaling
- ☐ Meditation

- ☐ Nourishing Foods
- ☐ Mindful Eating
- ☐ Went outside

- ☐ Moved My Body
- ☐ Expressed Gratitude
- ☐ Reflected on the day

AFFIRMATION OF THE DAY

REMEMBER

MORNING INTENTIONS

Morning Thoughts Feelings & Intuitions

How do you want to feel today?

What do you want to accomplish today?

EVENING REFLECTIONS

Evening Thoughts Feelings & Intuitions

How did you feel today?

What did you accomplish today?

GRATITUDE LIST

1.

2.

3.

Notes

Don't be afraid to ask for help if you need it. It shows great courage and strength

Date:

S / M / T / W / T / F / S

Today's Mood

☹ ☹ 😐 🙂 😃

Sleep time:_____to_____

Hours slept: _____

Self-care practices accomplished today

☐ Set intentions

☐ Journaling

☐ Meditation

☐ Nourishing Foods

☐ Mindful Eating

☐ Went outside

☐ Moved My Body

☐ Expressed Gratitude

☐ Reflected on the day

AFFIRMATION OF THE DAY

REMEMBER

MORNING INTENTIONS

Morning Thoughts Feelings & Intuitions

How do you want to feel today?

What do you want to accomplish today?

EVENING REFLECTIONS

Evening Thoughts Feelings & Intuitions

How did you feel today?

What did you accomplish today?

GRATITUDE LIST

1.

2.

3.

Notes

Believe in your journey, it's as unique as you are

Date:

S / M / T / W / T / F / S

Today's Mood

😞 😟 😐 🙂 😄

Sleep time:_____to_____

Hours slept: _____

Self-care practices accomplished today

- [ ] Set intentions
- [ ] Journaling
- [ ] Meditation

- [ ] Nourishing Foods
- [ ] Mindful Eating
- [ ] Went outside

- [ ] Moved My Body
- [ ] Expressed Gratitude
- [ ] Reflected on the day

AFFIRMATION OF THE DAY

REMEMBER

MORNING INTENTIONS

Morning Thoughts Feelings & Intuitions

How do you want to feel today?

What do you want to accomplish today?

EVENING REFLECTIONS

Evening Thoughts Feelings & Intuitions

How did you feel today?

What did you accomplish today?

GRATITUDE LIST

1.

2.

3.

Notes

You are fearlessly fabulous, don't forget that

Date:

S / M / T / W / T / F / S

Today's Mood

☹ ☹ 😐 🙂 😃

Sleep time:_____to_____

Hours slept: _____

Self-care practices accomplished today

- [ ] Set intentions
- [ ] Journaling
- [ ] Meditation

- [ ] Nourishing Foods
- [ ] Mindful Eating
- [ ] Went outside

- [ ] Moved My Body
- [ ] Expressed Gratitude
- [ ] Reflected on the day

AFFIRMATION OF THE DAY

REMEMBER

MORNING INTENTIONS

Morning Thoughts Feelings & Intuitions

How do you want to feel today?

What do you want to accomplish today?

EVENING REFLECTIONS

Evening Thoughts Feelings & Intuitions

How did you feel today?

What did you accomplish today?

GRATITUDE LIST

1.

2.

3.

Notes

Ask a friend why they love you and see that in yourself

Date:

S / M / T / W / T / F / S

Today's Mood

😣 😞 😐 🙂 😄

Sleep time:_____to_____

Hours slept: _____

Self-care practices accomplished today

☐ Set intentions
☐ Journaling
☐ Meditation

☐ Nourishing Foods
☐ Mindful Eating
☐ Went outside

☐ Moved My Body
☐ Expressed Gratitude
☐ Reflected on the day

AFFIRMATION OF THE DAY	REMEMBER

MORNING INTENTIONS

Morning Thoughts Feelings & Intuitions

How do you want to feel today?

What do you want to accomplish today?

EVENING REFLECTIONS

Evening Thoughts Feelings & Intuitions

How did you feel today?

What did you accomplish today?

GRATITUDE LIST

1.

2.

3.

Notes

Nurture yourself like you nurture others

Date:

S / M / T / W / T / F / S

Today's Mood

☹ ☹ 😐 🙂 😃

Sleep time:_____to_____

Hours slept: _____

Self-care practices accomplished today

☐ Set intentions
☐ Journaling
☐ Meditation

☐ Nourishing Foods
☐ Mindful Eating
☐ Went outside

☐ Moved My Body
☐ Expressed Gratitude
☐ Reflected on the day

AFFIRMATION OF THE DAY

REMEMBER

MORNING INTENTIONS

Morning Thoughts Feelings & Intuitions

How do you want to feel today?

What do you want to accomplish today?

EVENING REFLECTIONS

Evening Thoughts Feelings & Intuitions

How did you feel today?

What did you accomplish today?

GRATITUDE LIST

1.

2.

3.

Notes

Plan something to look forward to

Weekly Wins

Date:

S / M / T / W / T / F / S

WHAT FUN THINGS DID YOU DO THIS WEEK?

LIST 3 THINGS YOU LOVE ABOUT YOURSELF

WHAT HAVE YOU LEARNT ABOUT YOURSELF THIS WEEK?

Date:

S / M / T / W / T / F / S

Today's Mood

☹ ☹ 😐 🙂 😃

Sleep time:_____to_____

Hours slept: _____

Self-care practices accomplished today

- [ ] Set intentions
- [ ] Journaling
- [ ] Meditation

- [ ] Nourishing Foods
- [ ] Mindful Eating
- [ ] Went outside

- [ ] Moved My Body
- [ ] Expressed Gratitude
- [ ] Reflected on the day

AFFIRMATION OF THE DAY

REMEMBER

MORNING INTENTIONS

Morning Thoughts Feelings & Intuitions

How do you want to feel today?

What do you want to accomplish today?

EVENING REFLECTIONS

Evening Thoughts Feelings & Intuitions

How did you feel today?

What did you accomplish today?

GRATITUDE LIST

1.

2.

3.

Notes

Your past does not define you

Date:

S / M / T / W / T / F / S

Today's Mood

☹ ☹ 😐 🙂 😃

Sleep time:_____to_____

Hours slept: _____

Self-care practices accomplished today

☐ Set intentions
☐ Journaling
☐ Meditation
☐

☐ Nourishing Foods
☐ Mindful Eating
☐ Went outside
☐

☐ Moved My Body
☐ Expressed Gratitude
☐ Reflected on the day
☐

AFFIRMATION OF THE DAY

REMEMBER

MORNING INTENTIONS

Morning Thoughts Feelings & Intuitions

How do you want to feel today?

What do you want to accomplish today?

EVENING REFLECTIONS

Evening Thoughts Feelings & Intuitions

How did you feel today?

What did you accomplish today?

GRATITUDE LIST

1.

2.

3.

Notes

Give yourself a treat today

Date:

S / M / T / W / T / F / S

Today's Mood

☹ ☹ 😐 🙂 😀

Sleep time:_____to_____

Hours slept: _____

Self-care practices accomplished today

☐ Set intentions

☐ Journaling

☐ Meditation

☐

☐ Nourishing Foods

☐ Mindful Eating

☐ Went outside

☐

☐ Moved My Body

☐ Expressed Gratitude

☐ Reflected on the day

☐

AFFIRMATION OF THE DAY

REMEMBER

MORNING INTENTIONS

Morning Thoughts Feelings & Intuitions

How do you want to feel today?

What do you want to accomplish today?

EVENING REFLECTIONS

Evening Thoughts Feelings & Intuitions

How did you feel today?

What did you accomplish today?

GRATITUDE LIST

1.

2.

3.

Notes

Let your intuition guide the way

Date:

S / M / T / W / T / F / S

Today's Mood

☹ ☹ 😐 🙂 😃

Sleep time:_____to_____

Hours slept: _____

Self-care practices accomplished today

☐ Set intentions
☐ Journaling
☐ Meditation

☐ Nourishing Foods
☐ Mindful Eating
☐ Went outside

☐ Moved My Body
☐ Expressed Gratitude
☐ Reflected on the day

AFFIRMATION OF THE DAY	REMEMBER

MORNING INTENTIONS	EVENING REFLECTIONS
Morning Thoughts Feelings & Intuitions	Evening Thoughts Feelings & Intuitions
How do you want to feel today?	How did you feel today?
What do you want to accomplish today?	What did you accomplish today?

GRATITUDE LIST

1.

2.

3.

Notes

Stop putting so much pressure on yourself

Date:
S/M/T/W/T/F/S

Today's Mood
☹ ☹ 😐 🙂 😃

Sleep time:_____to_____
Hours slept: _____

Self-care practices accomplished today

☐ Set intentions
☐ Journaling
☐ Meditation

☐ Nourishing Foods
☐ Mindful Eating
☐ Went outside

☐ Moved My Body
☐ Expressed Gratitude
☐ Reflected on the day

AFFIRMATION OF THE DAY	REMEMBER

MORNING INTENTIONS	EVENING REFLECTIONS
Morning Thoughts Feelings & Intuitions	Evening Thoughts Feelings & Intuitions
How do you want to feel today?	How did you feel today?
What do you want to accomplish today?	What did you accomplish today?

GRATITUDE LIST

1.

2.

3.

Wrap yourself in love

Date:

S / M / T / W / T / F / S

Today's Mood

☹ ☹ 😐 🙂 😀

Sleep time:_____to_____

Hours slept: _____

Self-care practices accomplished today

☐ Set intentions

☐ Journaling

☐ Meditation

☐ Nourishing Foods

☐ Mindful Eating

☐ Went outside

☐ Moved My Body

☐ Expressed Gratitude

☐ Reflected on the day

AFFIRMATION OF THE DAY

REMEMBER

MORNING INTENTIONS

Morning Thoughts Feelings & Intuitions

How do you want to feel today?

What do you want to accomplish today?

EVENING REFLECTIONS

Evening Thoughts Feelings & Intuitions

How did you feel today?

What did you accomplish today?

GRATITUDE LIST

1.

2.

3.

Notes

Stop comparing yourself to others

Date:

S / M / T / W / T / F / S

Today's Mood ☹ ☹ 😐 ☺ 😃

Sleep time:_____to_____

Hours slept: _____

Self-care practices accomplished today

☐ Set intentions
☐ Journaling
☐ Meditation
☐

☐ Nourishing Foods
☐ Mindful Eating
☐ Went outside
☐

☐ Moved My Body
☐ Expressed Gratitude
☐ Reflected on the day
☐

AFFIRMATION OF THE DAY	REMEMBER

MORNING INTENTIONS

Morning Thoughts Feelings & Intuitions

How do you want to feel today?

What do you want to accomplish today?

EVENING REFLECTIONS

Evening Thoughts Feelings & Intuitions

How did you feel today?

What did you accomplish today?

GRATITUDE LIST

1.

2.

3.

Notes

If the ocean gets rough, grab your surf board and ride the waves

Weekly Wins

Date:

S / M / T / W / T / F / S

WHAT CHALLENGES DID YOU OVERCOME THIS WEEK?

HOW HAVE YOU BEEN KIND TO YOURSELF THIS WEEK?

WHAT CAN YOU RELEASE THAT YOU NO LONGER NEED?

Date: Today's Mood

S / M / T / W / T / F / S   ☹ ☹ 😐 🙂 😀

Sleep time:_____to_____

Hours slept: _____

Self-care practices accomplished today

☐ Set intentions   ☐ Nourishing Foods   ☐ Moved My Body

☐ Journaling   ☐ Mindful Eating   ☐ Expressed Gratitude

☐ Meditation   ☐ Went outside   ☐ Reflected on the day

☐   ☐   ☐

AFFIRMATION OF THE DAY	REMEMBER

MORNING INTENTIONS

Morning Thoughts Feelings & Intuitions

How do you want to feel today?

What do you want to accomplish today?

EVENING REFLECTIONS

Evening Thoughts Feelings & Intuitions

How did you feel today?

What did you accomplish today?

GRATITUDE LIST

1.

2.

3.

Notes

Learn to love your uniqueness. It's your superpower

Date:

Today's Mood

S / M / T / W / T / F / S ☹ ☹ 😐 🙂 😃

Sleep time:_____to_____

Hours slept: _____

Self-care practices accomplished today

☐ Set intentions   ☐ Nourishing Foods   ☐ Moved My Body

☐ Journaling   ☐ Mindful Eating   ☐ Expressed Gratitude

☐ Meditation   ☐ Went outside   ☐ Reflected on the day

☐   ☐   ☐

AFFIRMATION OF THE DAY

REMEMBER

MORNING INTENTIONS

Morning Thoughts Feelings & Intuitions

How do you want to feel today?

What do you want to accomplish today?

EVENING REFLECTIONS

Evening Thoughts Feelings & Intuitions

How did you feel today?

What did you accomplish today?

GRATITUDE LIST

1.

2.

3.

Notes

If you are struggling, remember how much you have overcome already

Date:

S / M / T / W / T / F / S

Today's Mood

😦 😕 😐 🙂 😃

Sleep time:_____to_____

Hours slept: _____

Self-care practices accomplished today

☐ Set intentions

☐ Journaling

☐ Meditation

☐ Nourishing Foods

☐ Mindful Eating

☐ Went outside

☐ Moved My Body

☐ Expressed Gratitude

☐ Reflected on the day

AFFIRMATION OF THE DAY

REMEMBER

MORNING INTENTIONS

Morning Thoughts Feelings & Intuitions

How do you want to feel today?

What do you want to accomplish today?

EVENING REFLECTIONS

Evening Thoughts Feelings & Intuitions

How did you feel today?

What did you accomplish today?

GRATITUDE LIST

1.

2.

3.

Notes

You can overcome challenges using your courage and resilience

Date:

S / M / T / W / T / F / S

Today's Mood

☹ ☹ 😐 🙂 😃

Sleep time:_____to_____

Hours slept: _____

Self-care practices accomplished today

☐ Set intentions
☐ Journaling
☐ Meditation

☐ Nourishing Foods
☐ Mindful Eating
☐ Went outside

☐ Moved My Body
☐ Expressed Gratitude
☐ Reflected on the day

AFFIRMATION OF THE DAY

REMEMBER

MORNING INTENTIONS

Morning Thoughts Feelings & Intuitions

How do you want to feel today?

What do you want to accomplish today?

EVENING REFLECTIONS

Evening Thoughts Feelings & Intuitions

How did you feel today?

What did you accomplish today?

GRATITUDE LIST

1.

2.

3.

Notes

Treat yourself with kindness

Date:

S / M / T / W / T / F / S

Today's Mood

☹ ☹ 😐 ☺ 😀

Sleep time:_____to_____

Hours slept: _____

Self-care practices accomplished today

- ☐ Set intentions
- ☐ Journaling
- ☐ Meditation

- ☐ Nourishing Foods
- ☐ Mindful Eating
- ☐ Went outside

- ☐ Moved My Body
- ☐ Expressed Gratitude
- ☐ Reflected on the day

AFFIRMATION OF THE DAY

REMEMBER

MORNING INTENTIONS

Morning Thoughts Feelings & Intuitions

How do you want to feel today?

What do you want to accomplish today?

EVENING REFLECTIONS

Evening Thoughts Feelings & Intuitions

How did you feel today?

What did you accomplish today?

GRATITUDE LIST

1.

2.

3.

Notes

The universe loves you unconditionally

Date:

S / M / T / W / T / F / S

Today's Mood

☹ ☹ 😐 🙂 😃

Sleep time:_____to_____

Hours slept: _____

Self-care practices accomplished today

☐ Set intentions
☐ Journaling
☐ Meditation
☐

☐ Nourishing Foods
☐ Mindful Eating
☐ Went outside
☐

☐ Moved My Body
☐ Expressed Gratitude
☐ Reflected on the day
☐

AFFIRMATION OF THE DAY

REMEMBER

MORNING INTENTIONS

Morning Thoughts Feelings & Intuitions

How do you want to feel today?

What do you want to accomplish today?

EVENING REFLECTIONS

Evening Thoughts Feelings & Intuitions

How did you feel today?

What did you accomplish today?

GRATITUDE LIST

1.

2.

3.

Notes

You are limitless

Date:

S / M / T / W / T / F / S

Today's Mood

☹ ☹ 😐 🙂 😀

Sleep time:_____to_____

Hours slept: _____

Self-care practices accomplished today

☐	Set intentions
☐	Journaling
☐	Meditation
☐	

☐	Nourishing Foods
☐	Mindful Eating
☐	Went outside
☐	

☐	Moved My Body
☐	Expressed Gratitude
☐	Reflected on the day
☐	

AFFIRMATION OF THE DAY

REMEMBER

MORNING INTENTIONS

Morning Thoughts Feelings & Intuitions

How do you want to feel today?

What do you want to accomplish today?

EVENING REFLECTIONS

Evening Thoughts Feelings & Intuitions

How did you feel today?

What did you accomplish today?

GRATITUDE LIST

1.

2.

3.

Notes

You are as courageous as a lioness

Weekly Wins

Date:

S / M / T / W / T / F / S

WHAT ARE YOUR TAKEAWAY THOUGHTS FROM LAST WEEK?

WHAT DID YOU DO TO LAUGH?

LIST 3 THINGS YOU'RE PROUD OF FROM LAST WEEK

Notes ♥

TODAY
I DECIDED TO SAY
YES TO ME.
I MIGHT EVEN TRY IT
TOMORROW!

- LW

Journal your thoughts on how you've changed through this process ♥

Notes ♥

Notes

Notes ♥

Notes

I hope you enjoyed this planner.
Why not keep your self-care going and purchase this
journal again from Amazon.

Make sure to visit
www.cosmicsoultherapy.co.uk to grab a self-care
freebie and check out my work.

Printed in Great Britain
by Amazon